✷Fr♆gm∞nts⊗

Tara Singh

Five Leaves Publications

✷Fr⚓gm∞nts⊗

Tara Singh

Published in 2025 by Five Leaves Publications
14a Long Row, Nottingham NG1 2DH
www.fiveleaves.co.uk
www.fiveleavesbookshop. co.uk

ISBN: 978-1-915434-32-6

Printed in Great Britain

Contents

Powerful, playful, innovative and questioning Fragments explores power imbalances, prejudices, pain, silencing and reclamation of the self in language and form that shifts with the uncertainty of untranslated memory. Tara Singh is a distinctive and essential new voice in British Poetry. These are poems that will and must have their histories and realities heard and seen.

Polly Atkin, author of *Much With Body*

This really took my breath away! Through technically inventive and emotionally raw poems, Tara Singh examines how the past can shape us and entrap us. Tender, visceral writing finds our narrator bruised, bloody, and still breathing in this collection of complex, confronting and incredibly beautiful poems. I'm really excited for more people to get to know Singh's writing!

Leanne Moden, author of *Get Over Yourself*

Delicate, dangerous, deadly — these poems strike at the heart with cutting precision. An incandescent debut.

Adam Lowe, author of *Patterflash*

Tara Singh's ✷Fr⚲gm∞nts⊗ revisits and subverts traditional folklore and religious text. These stylistically innovative and aesthetically refreshing verses enchant and surprise readers; they sing like shabads on Diwali nights, and dance like the flickering flames of diya lights. These poems interrogate family, belonging and queer desire in the Asian diaspora.

Hongwei Bao, author of *Self-Portrait as a Banana*

In Tara Singh's poetry, we tread the carefully sliced, vast expanses of emotion and experience alive in the intimacies of the tellings. Revealed are gaunt towerings of brutal racism, melted family machinery, the debris of glistening sensory surviving. These poems have such hungry angles that the world is keenly missing and will be compassionately richer for discovering.

The Mollusc Dimension, author of
The Weird & Wonderful Surviveries of Squid Horse

A beautiful searing breaking and remaking. The poems in this pamphlet are expertly deployed. A fantastic carving and re-carving of the self through verse. Works fantastically read contiguously or dipping in, a cartography of becoming. This is a brilliant collection of poems that sit well next to each other. I thoroughly enjoyed reading it.

PJ Samuels, contributor to
Sista! Anthology & Black and Gay in the UK

for my mother
for her mother
for her mother

'And of course I am afraid, because the transformation of silence into language and action is an act of self-revelation, and that always seems fraught with danger'

— Audre Lorde

✹ ⚓ ∞ ⊗

dissection of multitudes contained

take turns   snag skin
lift muscle   peel veins
pare fascia   reveal crimson

take soft
reach tenderest
tip me on your bedroom floor

fingers through ventricles
valves like rings
heartstrings in your palm

trace paths of travel
arteries veins nerves
know me inside out but

my lids are sealed
you'll never know
the colour of my eyes

The Zombie was Born

my teeth
sing for flesh
tongues
swallowed
in raging

a sea of medics

parts

I look at my blood
prophecy
something terrible
– *remember I loved you* –

/bi:p/

/bi:p/

/bi:p/

/bi:p/

/bi:p/

/bi:p/

unborn undead flesh
gasps wakes
grasps for
any body

InsideOutsideFugue

window-haunter
pull-away-contracter
✷∞⊗⚓
unsunned-spectre
a stroll outside &
cell walls liquefy
✷—∞—⊗—⚓
gravity unravels
✷——∞——⊗——⚓
DNA backbones break
✷————∞————⊗————⚓
-nuclei splinter mitochondria split cytoplasm spills-
✷——————∞——————⊗——————⚓
-plasm spills nuclei splinter mitochondria split cytoplasm-
✷————————∞————————⊗————————⚓
-chondria split cytoplasm spills nuclei splinter mitochondria split cyto-
✷——————————∞——————————⊗——————————⚓
-clei splinter mitochondria split cytoplasm spills nuclei splinter mitochondria split-
✷————————————∞————————————⊗————————————
-plasm spills nuclei splinter mitochondria split cytoplasm spills nuclei splinter mitoch
✷————————————∞————————————⊗————————————
all wanders end
inside where
brick walls hold
cells together
✷∞⊗⚓

✷Fr⚴gm∞nts⊗

✷ Instead of R@P& shout
FIRE curtains flame
village torched
⊗ refuse to swallow
pills ⚴ ache older
⊗ hide inside
dark recess of
It Never Happened
∞ banish all selves
✷ eat twin's twin ∞ snap
unspoken words back
⊗ beds bleed before
blackout ✷ crows
can have this carbon
⚴ return it as
cabbage butterflies
∞ heart misses
bloodbeat ⊗ empty
fist of air ✷ He is
embolism
⚴⊗∞✷
fingers print
whorls sear

○
⚴ Fawn
∞ Flight
⊗ Freeze
✷ Fight
○

part of that world

look at this house
it is not neat to end up with a girl who
doesn't seem to have a collection
of anything to make complete

there is no trove or treasure
no wonders or cavern
looking around you'd think
no child lives here at all

I'm the first there are no others
my scales are emerald satin
my hair is lush fire-red
I made a wish because I thought

I wanted to be where the people are
one day the girl decides
to take me to that place
what's it called? the bathroom

I'm ready to dance & swim but
she perches me on the edge of ugly coral
I want to ask Matey all my questions
he's gruff & unfriendly

I watch the bath being filled with
what do you call them? bubbles
they're flat
I wait for an invitation to play

the father comes in the girl seems
to forget I'm there I try to shut my eyes
then I remember my eyelids are plastic
the father leaves the girl seems to

forget what happened
she gets into her nightie
I try to say something but
I remember I'm not real

He summons while my mum does the dishes

She suds, draining rack
almost full. Carefully
balances the last bowl.

He casts citrus gem
clusters onto amber
charcoal. She squats

with her dustpan &
sweeps while frankincense
smoulders to musk smoke.

She listens to evening prayers
while his chants get louder
ॐ ह्रौं पिशाचस्याय स्वाहा

It arrives, flickers next to me
with scab skin with molten thorn
with seed fire with crack grin

with fast spins with black wings
with bleed pulse with howl eyes.
She wipes down the worktop

the smoke clears. He wipes
his face. She sweeps away
ashes. We don't eat dessert.

At night the weight of it sits
on the edge of my mattress.
My mum doesn't believe.

She says evil spirits
only become real when
you say they are.

ॐ ह्रौं पिशाचस्याय स्वाहा – *demon manifestation mantra*

The Bride is Prepared

Nani has been bathed
for breakfast the bride piles paper plates
with rose gulab jaman, sticky jalebi swirls
round orange ladoo, milk chocolate burfi.
Mami who eats too many samosas
& sneaks us JD coke arrives,
savours as she describes
her husband's grip on curves
as he fucks from behind.

The doorbell rings. She walks in
scarlet sari slung loose lithe body
milky-iris pulls out dining chair takes
hands in hers papery sunspot speckled
ink-blue veins cheap metal bangles
            chorus – she drops your hand.

            put salt under your pillow at night
            cast it to water each morning
            you will not die just yet but
            don't ever have your palm read again

Nani – grandmother
Mami – aunt

Watch Her Dissociate

Lunchtime chips linger
on shiny chevrons. Gaggles of girls
giggle in rounds. Legs crossed
feet bare – for a moment not there –
find myself in a pool of wet whole class
moves away like a snap of elastic
eyes ring as I uncross legs leave silence
& puddle & trail of footprints.
Ms Jonson wordless faded
lost property underwear rejected.
I go home damp PE kit still on
the body I can't feel. Papa's face
contorts, same routine yet again.
Soaped. Scrubbed. Rinsed out. Forgot.

Hysteria in duplex

Soft pink curves rose buds swollen syrup blood drops
the tremble of paper under her gossamer hand as she draws

> hurried ink prickles the scrap of paper with her hand's scrawl
> He slowly rips takes the uterus his smile reeks of game

The uterus in his hand he destroys with a hard hollow grin
my father tells me there is a sick womb & it's all my mother's

> He says I have no womb & the hysteria is all my mother's
> I believe him & wait for my penis to grow sterile & medicinal

I wait for my penis to grow from the lacking sour rancid place
but one day it is wounded into shrill howls of blood spurt

> The blood spills plaintive from my split shut body
> soiled & silent I stuff school toilet roll between my legs

in mirror pain I stuff my underwear with stolen white rags
soft pink curves rose buds swollen syrup blood drops

'Duplex' is a poetic form invented by Jericho Brown

The False Memory Fairy Tale

once upon
there was a house with dense air
in the house lived a father & daughter
very morning the father stood at the hob
and told the same story
there was once a bad daughter
who had wrong memories in her head
she spoke to people & told these tales
she had False Memory Syndrome
the daughter sometimes left her body
she wanted to talk
but the daughter was scared
she didn't know how to speak
when the daughter left the house
she was knotted up inside
then the daughter found someone
who had the job of listening
the daughter's memories came to life
some words got muffled & lost
when the story got tangled
her cheeks burned red as
she remembered hers and heard others
so many memories to share
the daughter put *False Memory* away
now she lives happily

a time
there were holes dug in the dirt
there was grey porridge
there was always grey porridge
every day was the same story
something *bad was happening*
something ***bad*** *was happening*
something bad ***was*** *happening*
something bad was ***happening***
in clouds evaporating away
skylarks lifted her to sing
she'd been stitched together in grey
mouth filled with stones lips sewn shut
she began believing in the world but
her words got lost in tangled yarn
she met a witch with a prism in their palm
they heard whispers from ghosts
in the healer's eyes like magpie's gold
her eggshell skin was pieced together
in milk voice & thistles & blood
fiery sun in clear blue
skylarks lifted them to sing
in a hearth hush of breath
the silence was over
ever after

untitled

I wonder how to teach
a displaced child to
know a part of

their body
hidden unlanguaged
found unnamed –

I wonder how I could
have made sense
when at five

she took me aside
& warned me –
I wandered in a muddle

of unmeaning unclear
understanding little
of what & where

My father never read

He skimmed through things in a few seconds & immediately proclaimed himself all-knower   My father said he got top marks in all exams with no need to read a single thing   My father never read instruction manuals directions recipes or side effects   My father signed contracts without reading them   My father made other people sign without letting them read   My father wouldn't read subtitles or subtext   My father never read a novel   When my mother tried to read my father clipped her face with the pages   My father never read a poem   My father laughed at people who wrote poems My father once saw me write a poem & told me to never write a poem again   My father made me write equations   My father only read the right hand corner of my school report   My father said he never read the letters about me   My father said he never read the letter from me   My father never read   My father is dead My father never reads anything so   My father won't ever read this   My father is alive & lives close enough to come & get me   Luckily my father never reads

(DON'T) SP--K

He was just hugging you –
nothing more –
Press-Lip-Custodian
Kohl-Eye-Sentry
Cross-Arm-Guard

Silenced away as if I
Horror-Film-Ghost-Child
only speak to accuse

[See faded photo from Long-Lost-Aunt]
My five-year-old shoulders hunch
his arm in loose hug my
little pony pyjama top creases
eyes to empty white gashes
smile to grimace as
I twist away

[Out of frame]
A constellation of adults
spectres swirl in whispers of
Izzat — Sharam —
DON'T SP--K

I spoke
now, I spook

Izzat – honour
Sharam – shame

(& so we bludgeon a cancer to death with a brick)

The night before your appointment we watch
him weave his wriggle fat body through the air

yap he jumps back swipes electric fast then lurches
you spot the gamy bald lump caught in his mouth

he chews spits catches, chews spits circles rowdy
riot & finally bored he walks away to piss in the bushes

We go look at the shivering stuccoed mass '*Is it dead*?'
you prod it tender with a twig, wonder if we should end

its misery, you pick up a brick & hurl, kick the lump
behind the fusty wheelie bin, walk away. Then we hear

a hollow echo resound I point my torch find the slick
stain it's left behind in the darkness waiting to be refound –

Samson

i

A violence so great that the only person who should cut is the mother

ii

The doughy pale sofa has sweat gathering at its pits
mangoes ripen on the kitchen worktop
the ceremony at the Golden Temple
wrapped marigold petals around
your crown now know who
you are not

iii

Osama
shouted by a white
van man –

iv

Forest Street Gurdwara
inside this place you could be
anywhere the world imported
from home but our living room
is where everything real happens
the beach scene on the wall watches
as you try to forget the clippers had teeth

v

like bat wings try to forget the cancer they cut out of you

vi

When your hair
grows back it feels
like lamb's ears

KNIFEBLOCK

FADE IN:
HIM, once a fat unhugged child whose father had one lung & two missing wives

SUPERIMPOSE:
A rat silhouette on the wall shrinks in the middle of an island that ate them alive. Outside an auction market waits to buy flesh bulks of meat. Centuries or seconds after they arrive look into the dark holes of *HER* face

TILT:
Kitchen tiles sing hollow anaemic light. *Knife #1* sleeps under *HER* pillow as *SHE* plays fugitive away from *HIM*. On the worktop a red dashed body of white loaf *HIS* fury ripped open with *Knife #2*

WIPE:
SHE gathers drugs like flowers *HER* life liberated in vials

MONTAGE:
(ravenous *HE* sucked pulp flesh left pit)

(policeman '*Did you say No*?' No, she says, but *HE* never asked)

(the next day *HE* returns to repair tears with a red coral ring from a pandit in the pub with a briefcase)

(pregnant too easily no longer worth gold *HER* wedding barter was thinly rolled silver)

JUMP CUT:
(*Knife #3* drops. *HER* labour begins)

FADE OUT –

Pandit – a Hindu priest or a wise man

Ichchadhari Naag

Summer swelter
steel pan bubbles
molten starch swamp
She stirs ink-black cloth
submerged it swells back up
a dark sea monster comes to life
She reaches deep into beast belly
captured and squeezed it bleeds
sticky translucent goo then you
wrap it around your head fearsome
creature slowly dries into shape of you;
spare glasses, black kohl smudge beard
slide into your shirt, slather your old spice
scent on my neck cradle your pagg –
absorber of forehead grease
scalp sweat I stop to sniff
the top of the hierarchy
I crown myself
I walk like you
I talk like you
I bully like you
I survive you

Ichchadhari Naag – 'Wishful Snake'; Indian folklore, a mythical cobra that can take any form

Pagg – in this case, a Kenyan style turban; a thin cotton cloth is soaked in starch, folded & wrapped around the head while warm. It is left on the head to dry. The same hard starched turban is worn daily for several months

The Summer Holiday I Decide to Fight

His elbows have jigsaw bends so
he can punch in a weak plastic way
a boy in Derby sold him to me for £1.99

Brother's vest, clammy eggs in tigger cup
gulp don't throw up burpee 1 2 3
Papa's pullup bar until dizzy

The Undertaker punches stones
I punch dried kala chana, my notebook
holds predictions good guys & bad

I make boy cousins fight, I always win
Baldish is the first to say fists clenched
'*boys & girls shouldn't play this way*'

neck flushed he points at my chest
'*you need to get a bra*' I lob the Undertaker
over the fence into bushes next door

My new notebook measures me
every day how many calories I take in
& how much I burn away

Kala chana – dried black chickpeas; these have an especially spiky rough surface

∞

Tell the Story that Saves Your Life

after Ocean Vuong

Cubicle curtain drawn I cave around a chest collapsed in cloudstorm heartbeats. Sterile breaths fill my ears as blue cotton healers won't listen when I remember it was an accident. I didn't mean for cells to blossom microbes like agar jelly, for capillaries to crack, for blood to collect, for brainfever to blush into summer evening sky. My body apologetic it convulsed; sorry that spine did not sprout wings when knees kissed concrete. A dart hits a vein, blood complains as it's pulled from its body. Lines switch and a bag of Save-Her-Life is decanted into vessels like wine; the flesh drinks with abandon but still the spirit abandons the flesh, it hangs itself from the cloudbloom stain of hospital ceiling tiles and asks the scurrying medics below, *Can you tell me my name*?

***

I cave around cloudstorm heartbeats
breaths fill my ears I remember
to blossom
to blush into summer evening sky. My body
did sprout wings when knees kissed
Life is decanted
into vessels like wine; the flesh drinks with abandon the spirit
hangs from the cloudbloom and asks
Can you tell me my name?

***

heartbeats
blossom
to blush
wings kiss
flesh spirit
asks
Can you tell me my name?

***

Heartbeats blossom to blush
Wings kiss flesh; Spirit asks
Can you tell me my name?

'Burning haibun' is a poetry form invented by torrin a. greathouse

//Fragmented//Fr⚓gm∞nt⊗d✹//✹r⚓⊗m∞n⚓⊗d✹//✹∞⚓⊗✹∞✹⚓⊗∞✹//

1972

For the numb & assimilated for Bobby Manny Vinny
who bled to stay, cut their hair gave up their names
turbans ripped from scalps
rejects told to Go Back Home
Paki-bashed their plans imploded to skinhead-fists
in The Motherland; burdened with British-Kenyan passports
on nervous flights, here to work, children sent to England
from the sleepless knots of a mother's nightmares
as expulsion from Uganda untethers

1947

With a single strike of ruler & ink
Punjab was butchered by British hand
At 83 heart thaws to tremble, she finally shares
– *Mata Pita took a ship, they escaped* –
10 years old her life sacrificed to a stranger made husband
as daggers slashed borders through neighbourhoods
limbs torn from beds homes lost streets wept
blood, overnight wife awaited the parents
who vowed to return, death followed the five babies
she birthed by her twenty-first year

1896

Hollowed out they settled in Kenya, built temples with
labour-worn bodies extracted from home, unpaid, abandoned –
The British took their work for free & abolished the word
Slavery in days of Plague, Lions & White Man's Promises
white eyes fixed profit on disposably brown bodies
3000 hostile miles away from home a Lunatic Line
takes its fodder signed with a cross hands forced
The British pushed them aboard ships in poverty
exiles from Punjab looked for work

Mata Pita – 'Mother-Father'; it is common & respectful to refer to parents collectively in Indian culture

Chardi Kala

Kidda?– he asks
Teek – he tells you

You remain silent –
His Teek –
No other answer an option –

3.23pm
UnseenPushKneesCrunchConcreteBloodiedFacePlaygroundGravel
GritSharpVinegarCrushedCrispsPouredOnJasmineOiledPlaitsFuck
ingPakiFuckingPakiFuckingPaki
Run –
Andrea holds hood
hear a tear
but these legs
have inherited how to
run –
into the road
car
swerves
horn
scolds
Stupid kids messing around

3.59pm
(You get home)

Kidda? – he asks
Teek – he tells you

You remain silent.
His Teek.
No other answer an option.

Chardi Kala – core concept in Sikhism; the practice of maintaining a consistently positive state of mind when faced with any adversity
Kidda – 'how's it going?'
Teek – 'well'

on your wedding night you slept on your mother's thread

****

Night-hum Nairobi generator
whitewash wall flickers with filament glow
quiver cast light encircles her embroidery
needle gripped soft in workhard thumb
shovels white shimmer thread
through hundreds of glossy pearls
from woven clusters gold curves emerge in
a spray of flowers from my Nani's imagination
her gift for your wedding day

****

We sit close on the bed
you share with him shrouded in her gift
'*Having you scares me*' – I listen. I run
my fingertip across the silk gilt petals
'*it's cruel to keep birds in cages. I can't fight*'
I carry on looking at the bedspread
notice how much my Nani's petals
look like golden wings in flight

****

The day she learned to ~~*cut*~~

with her incisors skin
from her lower
lip
as she folds she hides wants
to ~~*cut*~~ through the heavy
creased words
~~*cut*~~
metal blades gleam ~~*cut*~~ hard
slice skin a blanched
gaping gash
appears
empty ~~*cut*~~ fast fills with
urgent red so she ~~*cut*~~
another then
~~*cut*~~
her bedroom window open ~~*cut*~~
her confession onto the
street below ~~*I've*~~
~~*loved*~~
~~*Sophie   Melissa   Amber*~~
~~*Laura   Elena*~~
~~*Carly*~~
—

Everything Mapped

Window down –
traffic-hum taste fuel
skid-wheels kick-up
Nairobi cocoa-blush dust –
nobody cloud or drab
everybody equator –
red-rose-rhodos
lilac-breasted-rollers
corn-yolk-sunsets –
whole life woven
speak technicolour –

Window up//
Cold glass transition//
Here everybody cloud//
Roads dictate//
White strikes
mark out gloom//
Signs shout arrows//
Red triangles glare//
Everything Map//
England bleached
white bread//
muffled coughs//

Fulcrum Story

From farmerwalas
rickshawalas
constructionwalas

how did I
unlabouring descendant
end up with knees
like these

My good knees saved me

I got away
rode a bike on the A46
with demon lorries
scorching my skull

Most days now
I'm thanking pink pills
to get me up stairs

some days
I almost believe
there are *5 simple tricks*
to fix your bad knees forever

but when my kneecaps scream
I know for sure
I will never be able
to matha take
jump a fence or run away again

Farmerwala - farm labourer
Rickshawala - labourer who pulls a rickshaw
Constructionwala – labourer in construction
Matha take – to prostrate on knees in worship

Razor

~ mtoto umleavyo ndivyo akuavyo
the way a child is raised is the way it grows
~ mtoto akilia wembe mpe
when a child cries for a razor, give it to him

You had three but
were paid to look after me
affectionately your mtoto
for the workday

Feed me ugali
teach me kuku says kuuu
mbwa says bow-wow
cradle me away
from glass shatter shards
whisky punch tears
swaddle me on hush breast –
walk away
once your shift
is over.

I grew to know how to be left
I can't remember crying for a razor
but I must have done
it feels like somebody gave me one.

Mtoto – child
Ugali – maize porridge
Kuku – chicken
Mbwa – dog

Bedtime Sonnet

Voices crack as hours leave in mother tongue lost
to me. I skip behind the beat as we invoke into the dusk,
net spiders on my wall, words grow resonant as oak.
I grip a tract in black & red, spiritual paper sword in soft

breath incantation to protect. ਦੁਸਟ ਦੂਤ ਪਰਮੇਸਰਿ ਮਾਰੇ, we intone,
mud to lotus bloom, but faith fills the room with darker corners.
Silver white of chunni on her head speaks of mourners,
the fall into night weaves deeper inside marrow-bone.

Say the right words to keep you safe, say them throat sore,
it's bedtime. She stops, sweeps supplication from salwar kameez.
In my room she leaves behind white mala toward the freeze,
as slash of night opens to wounds between dusk & dawn tear,

she tucks in white sheets deadquiet creepsteps nightly tread.
My grandmother knows why I can't sleep in my bed.

ਦੁਸਟ ਦੂਤ ਪਰਮੇਸਰਿ ਮਾਰੇ – Sikh prayer: 'The Transcendent Lord strikes down the Wicked and the Evil'
Chunni – traditional long chiffon scarf
Salwar kameez – traditional baggy tunic & trousers
Mala – prayer beads

Mummy

I. Announce
White man appears
stinking mouth breathes
car windows steam
– Dirty Brown Paki

II. Embalm
Foul brown
my Paki's Hand on dirty hall floor
pull away secrete in pocket

III. Organ Removal
Raise my Paki's Hand
in class
Blonde Miss Leigh points
– You. Read.
– 'The Egyptians would embalm their dead'
(except I pronounce 'dead' 'dad')

– Again
– 'The Egyptians would embalm their dad'

– Say it properly – 'Dead' as in 'Fled…Red…Bled…'

– […]

– What's the matter? Cat got your tongue?

IV. Desiccate Body
Whole class watches
feel less than human
nothing

V. Wrap Body
Bound
never offer
my Paki's Hand up again

VI. **Final Procession**

Drop dad. Dad as a doornail. Roll over & play dad. Dad men tell no tales.
Dad & buried. Dad to the world. Dad end. Dad silence.
From my cold, dad hands –

Passportless Minor Refuses Beef Pie

The border flutters
I stay still while
my brother flies

I hide behind graffiti walls
shrink from any blue siren
pose like a citizen

I visit sticky ears Laura for
chips mushy peas & –
            'but I can't eat beef

I'm loud in a crumpled front room –
            '…we drink milk from cows like we drink milk from mothers…
            & you would never eat your mother would you?'

mildew & sourness
when he laughs teeth
gravy brown

So I eat
my first British beef sweaty
unchewable resignation

Laura's dad's eyes are saws
his laugh powdery as
the corners of his lips

            'I thought your god didn't want you to
            eat cows? …Oh, don't cry
            it's just banter!'

so I put myself away
just like an over-seen
invisible person should

dsm

dsm never lets you see the soles of her feet
dsm is there the night the devil is on your knees
dsm says if god ever talks back then we call it
dsm loves to take you prey into her white blessèd arms
dsm rocks you to haze of scientific story's clear bright ray
dsm tells you the tale of serotonin as if it were fact
dsm sprays your mouth with a confetti of pills
dsm lies bitterly against the undigested tract of stray memories
dsm leaves your skull cracked open to pigeons
dsm says she gave you the roadmap to normal
dsm adores your intrusive thoughts & grasps them like bouquets
dsm uses your new symptoms as foreplay
dsm peels skin from your eyes to see what's underneath
dsm has her fingers down your throat reaching for decay
dsm doesn't want to hurt you but '*If I stop now you will be sorry*'
– so you stay

dsm – Diagnostic and Statistical Manual of Mental Disorders

O

Survival Messages

1. Life is hard
2. Tears are weak
3. Silence is strong
4. Stay invisible
5. Nobody cares
6. Never get attached
7. Don't ask for help
8. Food is not promised
9. Safety is a suitcase under the stairs
10. Rest is dangerous

Survival Messages – when our predecessors have lived under oppressive circumstances, they can develop 'survival messages' that may be passed on from one generation to the next. While these messages may have helped protect earlier generations, they may be less helpful to later generations.

There is emerging evidence that the effects of intergenerational trauma can be repaired for future generations when we consciously become aware of the survival messages we have absorbed from those who came before us.

Survival Messages (reboot)

1. Life is recreated with every soft landing coaxed out of the concrete of each hard fall
2. Tears have claws, know all the best watering holes, can pick out a predator for miles & are never weak
3. Silence is Waheguru whispered strong into every Urdu letter your Punjabi grandfather wrote his lover over the border
4. Staying in flight is not the same as being invisible, your mirror can see you even if you don't look up
5. ~~No~~Yourbody caresses your blood into twists of nucleotide maps for a future you have already broken time to live into
6. Never abandon your youngest self, get them attached to your wisest guide rope, lead them forward into this moment
7. Don't forget, when you finally made that call asking for help you dared to reach from the dark & found a hand to hold
8. Food is a grain of rice pressed between the pages of an atlas, served by hands that do not shake – even good food scalds your pot if left unpromised
9. Safety is sweet ghee from prasad on your palm, your grandmother's surmadani tracing your eyes & a suitcase filled with smarts under the stairs
10. Rest is found under grass or as ashes – but also in beds; Naps are dangerous to those who want to own us

Waheguru – the name of God in Sikhism, chanted as a mantra
Prasad – a sacred sweet offering in Sikhism, made with wheat flour, ghee & sugar. It's always served warm & is traditionally offered in the palm of one's hand, cupped to receive the blessing
Surmadani – traditional ornate bronze container used to store & apply surma (powdered kohl eyeliner) this object has deep roots in South Asian culture

The Therapist's Chair Walks In

spacetime twitches
glitches into bruises
        you are ready to
        leap invisible every
time you imagine a
creak from the chair –
        hooded not ready to see
        you draw your claws
deep try to perch light
enough for flight with
        delicate bones you dart
        back into dark with
the sureness of a fox on
a floodlit football pitch –
        a small sassy dog
        raises an eyebrow &
the chair's arms are
filled with blood
        oranges cups of golden
        chamomile a box of paints
under the seat is an
empty tin of shortbread –
        you are so taken by
        the unveiling of care
you almost don't notice
the cloth is worn threadbare –
        still you meet every week
        paint the chair's feet
orange as it blows feathers
at your mind

in a coma I roll a dice with Death

hovering over my hospital bed
cold bony fingers tumble chance
a cousin cries angular tears
on bedside chair an uncle bored
with glassy stare my mother fades
my father walks away
    we play
    day 1 - she wins with scar book
    day 2 - I win with people here
    day 3 - is hers in pills, vodka (‘*your summons like wedding bells*’)
    day 4 - I win with mornings I want to be woken
    day 5 - we lose with Old Man Time
    day 6 - Death decides she’s done playing for my life &
                                        I wake up
                              to a bright yellow omelette
                                   on a cheap china plate
                         I swoop on the flamboyant egg
                                the most delicious thing

O

Holy

shabads
sung on high
into Diwali night
down here 100
candles dance 1000
bright church rafters
reflect in diya light
Offering flame you murmur
– move your finger through –
I do fast enough to not feel
I want to impress you so I drip
hot wax on skin watch you
flinch I want to test you
we dare from shadow in
to light as our shabad
burns to Diwali

N
i
g
h
t

Shabads – poetic verses from Sikh holy text, sung during worship
Diya – a traditional oil lamp, made of baked clay

praise path

someone grey once
tapped all the gur
from my blood

I lack sweetness now
but still praise
gurdwaras even

when doors are shut
bring me back
for langar

I stopped
eating roti but
still praise saag

may you all be iron
praise in Punjabi
if your parents

gifted it with
unlanded accent
praise giddha

clapping light
as I reap
the harvest

praise ancestral as soil
my farmer shadow
finding the home

land in my body
this is my path
I'll wear it out

Path – pronounced 'pa-ath'; a daily regime of a devotional recitation of Sikh holy scripture; connecting with the divine through the spoken word
Gur – very sticky sweet blocks of palm sugar, popular in South Asia
Langar – a community kitchen found in every gurdwara, introduced by the founder of Sikhism Guru Nanak. He encouraged offering free meals to everyone who visited, regardless of their caste, gender or wealth.
Roti & Saag – a very traditional, culturally significant Punjabi dish; to not eat this is to admit you have lost touch with your roots
Giddha – traditional Punjabi folk dance which involves joyful clapping & singing

Acknowledgements

With gratitude
to Five Leaves for the open window
to Pippa for the care-full editing
to Duncan for being my therapist's chair
to Leanne for leading me to Paper Cranes & poetry
to PJ, Hongwei & Adam for being BPOC Flourish
to Speak the Word & Shaded Writers for being my poetry home
to Polly & Open Book for being poetry anchors
to Ruth for introducing me to all the queer poets
to my mother & brother for letting me tell all the secrets

Five Leaves New Poetry

Five Leaves presents a series of debut poetry pamphlets by East Midlands writers, showcasing the exciting range of emerging talent from our region.

1. *She Will Allow Her Wings* **Jane Bluett**
   978-1-915434-09-8, 40 pages, £7, June 2023
2. *Beyond Caring* **Trish Kerrison**
   978-1-915434-10-4, 40 pages, £7, September 2023
3. *North by Northnorth* **Elvire Roberts**
   978-1-915434-12-8, 44 pages, £7, December 2023
4. *The Stories In Between* **Teresa Forrest**
   978-1-915434-11-1, 32 pages, £7, December 2023
5. *Keep All the Parts* **Roy Young**
   978-1-915434-13-5, 34 pages, £7, March 2024
6. *Relief Map* **Jan Norton**
   978-1-915434-14-2, 33 pages, £7, March 2024
7. *New Uses for a Wand* **Fiona Theokritoff**
   978-1-915434-16-6, 40 pages, £7, June 2024
8. *You Worry Too Much* **Nathan Fidler**
   978-1-915434-17-3, 32 pages, £7, June 2024
9. *Kindling* **Julie Burke**
   978-1-915434-19-7, 44 pages, £7, September 2024
10. *Remembering* **Julie Gardner**
    978-1-915434-20-3, 40 pages, £7, September 2024
11. *Full Body Reclaim* **Caroline Stancer**
    978-1-915434-25-8, 40 pages, £7, December 2024
12. *Rainbow Candles* **Tony Challis**
    978-1-915434-31-9, 38 pages, £7, September 2025
13. *Fragments* **Tara Singh**
    978-1-915434-32-6, 49 pages, £7, September 2025

All pamphlets can be ordered from our websites.

Five Leaves Publications/Bookshop
14a Long Row, Nottingham NG1 2DH **0115 837 3097**
info@fiveleaves.co.uk **bookshop@fiveleaves.co.uk**
www.fiveleaves.co.uk **www.fiveleavesbookshop.co.uk**